INTUITION

Intuition is Calling - Please Answer or Text Back.

Sabrina Brightstar

Intuition is Calling - Please Answer or Text Back.

Communicating With Your Guides and Higher Self

ISBN: 978-1-947125-08-7

Author's website www.SabrinaBrightstar.com

Dedicated to Moriah and Andre'

Table of Contents

A Key To Inward Cognition - Intuition

I want to start this journey into the spiritual realm with a true story a friend shared with me. This friend was an animal lover, in particular, birds of prey. He was more than a bird enthusiast, appreciative of beautiful plumage or enthralling avian behaviors. My friend was a bit embarrassed to admit to me that he felt some sort of preternatural kinship with birds of prey. In fact, he was reluctant to share the story because he was concerned I might perceive his abiding affection for birds to be...well nuts, really.

Anyway, he stumbled onto an opportunity to 'own' a hawk as the previous owner didn't have time to attend to its needs. With bird in hand, he began to experience emotions quite unfamiliar to him. For the first time, he perceived a dimension to life that had previously been hidden to him. This he attributed to the hawk, with which he found himself forming a strong bond.

He built a sprawling enclosure for the raptor, three times the size of its previous accommodations. Every day he would spend upwards of an hour with this majestic creature, hand feeding it and attempting to train the bird to fly to his arm. As months marched past, though, the relationship between bird and man assumed a different tone. Moments spent in the enclosure became dominated by piercing stares from the hawk. These stares he described as soul penetrating. Subsequently, a prolonged period of restive nights began. His sleep was tormented by complex dreams in which the hawk was the principal protagonist. Every night a new dream would follow, each narrative more developed than the last. At first, he dismissed these dreams as night-time manifestations of guilt pangs over his imprisonment of a creature not meant to be caged.

1

However, he eventually grew to accept the dreams were actually more significant than fevered constructs of the mind. They were communications. Each time he laid his head down, messages were broadcast in his mind. These messages spoke to a gathering disturbance, not of mind or body, but what he felt was his soul. He interpreted these communications as projections into his mind of an unseen force, represented invariably by the hawk in his care.

He resolved to free the creature, not merely to unshackle himself from ongoing nocturnal anguish, but to answer an undeniable call embodied in this regal creature he had come to revere. On the day of the bird's liberation, he fed it one last time, opened the cage door and stood back. The hawk stared at him for what seemed like an age, then flew down to the ground and stood momentarily assessing what was happening. It walked tentatively to the cage door and then, in a blur of feathers, escaped to a nearby tree. From that perch, my friend recounted, the bird looked down on him, again, eventually disappearing into the sky. Dreams involving his hawk continued, but their tone had been dramatically transformed.

I count my friend as having been one of the most unbending spiritualism skeptics out there. After his experience, though, with what he accepted was far more than a mere bird, his eyes and heart were opened to messages to which they had been previously closed. Following his conversion, if you will, he remarked, "It is difficult to explain what I experienced to people who aren't equipped with the language to comprehend. I was one of them myself before this language was shared with me through the conduit of my dreams."

It is this "language", its communication and communicators that this book seeks to illuminate.

In this instance, there was a 'knowing' which my friend couldn't quite put his finger on. Intuition was knocking at his door some time before he answered. Intuition is defined as a natural ability to know something without the benefit of proof or evidence.

Under the guiding hand of intuition, people are often motivated to act a certain way without fully understanding why. Learning how to respond to intuition and interpret its language can open pathways to truly fulfilling experiences.

Machines Talk - Technology

Intuition is the direct link to knowing or following a knowing. If you received a call from Intuition would you answer? Many people miss and dismiss calls from Intuition. They assume Intuition is fake news, unimportant information or too subtle to make a difference.

What if Intuition is a real live resource center? What if Intuition is a field or space of information to assist and support you? What if you have access to infinite wisdom?

Technology is similar to intuition. We know technology allows us to resource information, gather data and get answers. Most humans are comfortable communicating with machines . Computers, laptops and cellphones are all man made machines that allow communication and connection.

Today it is common to see people talking to themselves. Let me explain this more clearly. We see people who appear to be talking to themselves. We see a person alone in the car talking. We see a solo person walking down the street talking. We understand technology today, so we assume they have in an ear piece and they are communicating with someone via technology.

If you were unaware of technology and their gadgets, you might think that person alone in the car, who appears to talking to the air is crazy. A person without awareness of technology might judge someone as nuts, strange or wacko.

Does being unaware of technology make that conversation null and void? Does the communication and connection become insignificant because the person observing does not understand it?

What if everyone can resource an invisible field of information? Would you be open to the possibilities of communication with the unseen?

If Intuition called your cell phone, would you answer or text back?

Guides

Recently I was asked about guides. The question was: "Are my guides aspects of my higher self or multidimensional self?"

Well, that's a great question. People generally believe guides are invisible beings assigned to offer support, protection and guidance. Some perceive them as angels or highly evolved, disembodied, spiritual beings. Others believe they are deceased relatives looking out for them. Then, there are those who believe they are paired with animal guides (like my friend and his hawk).

Instead of pondering on who your guides are, let's examine the location of the question. Okay, I know I lost you there for a moment so I'll explain. It really goes to the vibration location of the question. If you're coming from a position that consciousness is separate, then your belief that your guides are separate beings is perfectly reasonable. In the third dimension, most of us have been inculcated with the ideology of every living being existing as a separate identity.

In other dimensions, however, it's quite different. The collective consciousness espouses the notion that we are all one, that all consciousnesses are interconnected. This concept is hinged on the idea that all identities are gathered under the same umbrella. As such, they are all connected and a part of the ONE. One great river is the sum total of many individual streams. These streams come from different sources, but are ultimately one collective stream. Let's try another analogy. Imagine a tree if you will. All the branches exist individually, yet they are all connected to the tree trunk. Therefore, they are all a part of the ONE tree.

For some people, this concept makes perfect sense and is an

accurate representation of their experiences. Others, though, will find this way of thinking far too sinewy to process.

If your point of view or your thought form is operating from the I am One with All That Is vibration, one would say your guides are aspects of yourself, or multidimensional self. If, however, your point of view or thought form is operating from a linear, three-dimensional vibration, one would say your guides are separate beings.

In this instance, both answers and conclusions are accurate. Being aware of the location of your vibration (frequency) helps you understand your beliefs. Awareness also helps you appreciate why others might have different beliefs or answers to the same question. This isn't a simple matter of determining who is right or wrong. Conscious evolution is all about determining your vibrational location and allowing others to follow their vibrational path.

The question of who is right or wrong is asked in a polarity vibration. In polarity vibration or frequency, the answers are black or white. In a spiral, everything is included. It's a vibration or frequency that is non linear. As such, all answers can be right at the same time. There is no one truth.

What Is The Difference Between Polarity Vibration and Spiral Vibration?

Polarity or spiral vibrations are terms used to describe states of being. Two people can physically be in the same location, yet in completely different vibration spaces. A vibration space can constitute your mental body, emotional body, energetic body, spiritual body and your physical body. The word location, used in the spiritual context, doesn't refer to a specific geographic place on the planet. That's why it is entirely possible to have two people standing in the exact same location and having two different experiences.

Polarity vibration is a space in which labels are affixed to events. Experiences and behaviors come from a place of good or bad, right or wrong, good or evil. In this space, there are opinions and definitions about what situations and experiences mean. It's a place with a fixed point of view, a wholly logical vibration. Information is gathered and reported based on physical, tangible evidence. It's a place of supreme order, with all things having a dawn and a dusk, a beginning and an end. Things unfold in a linear sequence. This is a space where comparisons live and people tend to measure against one another. Hierarchies in race, economics, education, religion, gender, titles find their oxygen here. Some call this space 3D or the 3rd dimension.

Spiral vibration, by contrast, is a space of unlimited possibilities and multiple realities. This is a space of fluidity. There are no rigid points of view. Definitions are malleable and can change rapidly. Experiences and events can be observed without judgment or definition of their meaning. Information can flow in either a linear sequence or a random order. Time and space are lucid. Communication and connection to others can happen on a variety of planes and across many different pathways. It's a location where there is access to unlimited information and resources. One can be an individual consciousness, a collective consciousness, or both simultaneously. It's a space comprising both physical and non-physical experiences. This place is often referred to as a higher vibrational space, like 5D. I prefer the term "wider vibrational space." It is all-inclusive, honoring and validating all points of view.

Each moment gives us the option to be aware of our now state of being. We can be conscious, operating from a polarity point of view or a spiral point of view. Most of us flit in and out of these vibration spaces. Initially, when people become conscious of the different vibrations and believe in them, they try to stay cocooned in the spiral vibration. In this vibration, one feels and experiences freedom, joy, ease and acceptance.

The polarity vibration judges the spiral vibration as either non-existent, or as a superior location. From the spiral vibration, there is no judgment of where a person chooses to experience their now state of Being. The spiral vibration appreciates the value of experiencing the polarity vibration. Additionally, the spiral vibration knows no point of vibration is permanent. Each moment is a new, now moment to make a choice.

It's my personal belief that all aspects of my multidimensional self exist to support, and assist me on my journey of evolution, exploration and experience.

Communicating With Guides Or Multidimensional Self

There are many things to consider before delving into connecting with your guides and tapping into your higher self. You should first ask yourself whether you believe it will be easy to establish links with your guides or multi-dimensional aspects. What do you think that conversation will sound and feel like? Are you working with preconceived ideas of what interactions with your guides will be like? How open are you to a variety of methods that your multi-dimensional aspects or guides use to communicate?

These questions are important because, in some instances, our beliefs make establishing contact more difficult. For example, if you believe that connecting to your guides is difficult or you aren't confident in communicating with your multidimensional self, this creates a field that supports your beliefs. Beliefs are more powerful than we give them credit for. Consequently, one of the fastest ways to connect to your guides is to be aware of your beliefs and adopt an open attitude towards new beliefs that will make the connection effortless.

The next step is to scour your mind to determine whether you have any preconceived ideas of how that communication will manifest. If you are starting out with an expectation that the connection will be an audible voice speaking in English, perhaps saying, "Hello Sabrina, my name is Zoriah, I am your guide" then you will only be looking for this type of interaction. That's not to say this sort of connection isn't going to happen, but an awareness and willingness to embrace multiple ways of communication is important.

Have you ever had a conversation with a baby? I know what you're thinking, "Silly rabbit, babies can't talk!"

This, though, is precisely the point. We often communicate with babies in nonlinear words. There are smiles, we make baby sounds that might seem ridiculous in the company of others, and there are also lullabies. These are all valid communications, connections without the use of conventional language and sentences. In reaction to our facial gestures, cooing and soft singing, babies chortle, kick their tiny feet furiously and even muster a giggle; the connection is made.

Imagination is a vital tool in helping you to grasp the multiple ways your guides may connect with you.

Communicating Without Words

One tool to help you realize the multitude of ways your Guides may connect with you, is to imagine you are nonphysical, how would you communicate with a human who can't see you? How would you catch someone's attention to let them know you are trying to communicate?

Write a list of all the ways you might try to connect. Have your friends write a list. You will notice you may think of some of the same ideas as well as ideas no one else has written on their list. This demonstrates the point that connection is individualized. Your Guides may communicate and connect with you in a way no one else experiences.

The awareness that there are a variety of ways for your Guides to communicate with you, really opens the door. Once you recognize the multiple ways Guides can communicate, you become more aware and more prepared to catch the connections/conversations.

Random Bits and Pieces

Another key piece of insight is to recall Guides live in a spiral vibration. Many humans are inside a polarity vibration. What does that mean? It means inside the spiral vibration, space and time are lucid. Events and experiences do not necessarily unfold in a linear sequence. For example, imagine hearing a story. In the polarity vibration the story is told in order. There is a beginning, a middle and an end, a sequential order. In a spiral vibration, information and communication can be random. One might receive pieces of the end of the story, before one hears or catches the beginning of the story.

Being aware your communication with your Guides can be shared in random bits and pieces, helps you stay open and fluid rather than draw an open and shut conclusion. Gather the data and let the whole story present itself to you in whatever time frame it shows up.

Sometimes I hear people say they feel their Guides are not communicating or they have lost communication. One reason this can be happening is the human mind is not looking or prepared to look for random intel. It is easy to dismiss communication when it does not come in a linear order or in an expected format.

I know for myself, this insight changed the way I was able to connect. I started realizing all pieces of connection and conversation were significant, even though I was often puzzled by the meaning. I found with time, the pieces came together. Sometimes it even took years for whole insights and understandings to land.

Instead of dismissing the strange or bizarre pieces of connection I was receiving, I began to write them. I would anchor the experiences and information with writing or story sharing. I discovered other information would be shared later and eventually I could see a whole picture. I also realized other humans might have pieces of the puzzle and, by sharing my experiences, I would discover more meaning. When we exchange experiences, we often discover our stories are entangled or interwoven.

Get Unplugged

Realizing that communication is always happening helped me honor all the pieces. This lead to my discovering the meaning and benefit of all types of communication. One way to achieve this is to disconnect from the trappings of modern life for a while. Today's societies are so wired and physically attached to their smart phones and computers that people scarcely recognize that they are less connected that they have ever been before! If you relinquish your attachment to the addictions of technology, you clear the psychic clutter that keeps you from hearing your guides.

The demands of contemporary society are such that we barely have time to hear anything other than schedules, deadlines, reports and financial obligations. If, from the time we awake to the time we collapse with exhaustion into our beds every waking moment is occupied with the hurly burly of life, how will we hear our Guides? It is important to carve out time every day to tune into our Guides, to receive the messages they are sending.

Spontaneous Hits

I get communication in the form of inspired action. For no particular reason, I am inspired to go somewhere or to talk to someone and I hear a piece of information that adds to my story. It's true, not all spontaneous urges are created equal. Some people get an irresistible urge to rob a liquor store, or eat an entire pizza alone. There are some urges you can easily ignore. Others, however demand your attention, and I'm willing to bet that you'll know what they are and when they come.

Sometimes there's that voice that's telling you to get in your car and take a drive to a scenic location. Other times you will feel a pull to go to the park or head out to the coast. When these urges pop up, it is a good idea to follow them. When you yield to spontaneity, you start to become more in tune with your Guides.

Open To Possibilities

I find I often get communication in the form of an image or visual in my mind's eye. I get communication during dreams. I get communication with feelings. Out of the blue, I can simply just know something. It may not make sense to anyone else, or it may not be believable to anyone else. I have learned to pay attention to the diverse ways communication shows up. I have learned to trust my connection is unique to me. I create pathways for me to be able to receive.

The more I am aware that I am having connections with my Guides or, as I like to label it, aspects of my Multidimensional Self, the more conversations I hear. When I say hear conversations, I am not only referring to hearing with auditory sound, I mean hear, in the sense I catch it. It lands in my Field. The more I connect and become aware, the more that constant connection happens. The wider my consciousness becomes, the more I can receive and participate in multidimensional connections/communications.

My Story of Courage

Here is a personal story on how I started to learn communication with my multidimensional Self. I share this story in my book Stories From A Starseed.

One of the first telepathic messages that dropped in my field was "stones are radios". This happened in the spring of 2010. I thought it was a strange and bizarre piece of information. It made zero sense to me.

For some reason, I kept hearing in my head, "tell people, tell people." What, I thought? Why would I share a message with people that makes no sense to me?

I felt like I was being tested - sort of like an initiation test. Would I be brave enough to share this strange and unusual message?

I had a sense if I passed this initiation test, I would be given more information so I decided to tell my sister.

I had no concerns she would judge me. When I shared the message with her, she instantly started laughing and making jokes. She playfully suggested I wrap rocks for Christmas presents. She even suggested that when my family asked, why did we get a rock as a present, I could tell them, they are not rocks, they are radios. You can get rid of your cell phone and use your rock.

We laughed; it was funny! Then she started making jokes about my needing a "white jacket". That hurt my feelings. I had not expected anyone might joke that I am going insane.

A few days later, I was on a Skype group call with my mastermind group. We each took turns sharing. When it came my turn to talk, I kept hearing in my head, "tell them, tell them."

These were women whom I really admired and respected and I thought there is no way I am sharing this message with them. Yet, when I opened my mouth to share, it came spilling out. I told them I had gotten a telepathic message that stones are radios.

Silence.

No one said a word. I could just feel the energy of the call changed, I felt embarrassed. Then one of the women, Tracy, said she thought it made sense. What? How does it make sense, I asked her? She replied that she had read somewhere that, during the time of Atlantis, they used stones for communication. She thought it was crystals stones. She suggested I google crystals and Atlantis. I felt relieved. Not only did she save me from feeling like a fool, she also gave me a piece of the puzzle.

After the group call, I googled the information. You cannot even begin to imagine my shock, when I found an article that explained how Atlanteans used crystals stones to create radio waves. The article confirmed the exact message I had received. My confidence and trust in myself instantly started to grow.

I learned many important lessons from this experience.

One, I realized just because something doesn't make sense to me, that doesn't mean it isn't true or accurate. I also learned the importance of co-creating with others.

Our multidimensional family works together to help each other understand, digest and receive information. Thanks to myself for having the courage to share the message, Tracy was able to give me an important piece of the puzzle.

We each bring important pieces of the puzzle and when we share what we sense or know, we help each other.

The last thing I learned and have really come to understand on a deep level is the importance of sharing or expressing information that is dropped in our field. When we share and express insights, messages, sensing, and ideas, we open up more space in our field.

If we dismiss and ignore these hits and downloads, our field stays full. Imagine a container, if the container is never decanted, there is no room for new information to land. The container can start to feel stale and stagnant.

Have you ever felt "stuck"? This can be an indicator information wants to be released. There are multiple ways to release energy. Energy (consciousness) needs to move. It needs fluidity to ebb and flow. We can move energy with storytelling, writing, painting, building, dancing, singing, etc.

How we process energy can be an indicator of how ready we are to receive and evolve. If we are not comfortable with insights or downloads that drop in our Field, it can be an indicator we are not ready to expand in our multidimensional journey. In a sense a test is given, but what I understand today, the test is not given from an outside source. The test is given from YOU. An aspect of your multidimensional self is checking in with you to see if you are ready and available. This allows your journey to unfold with more balance and integration.

The Language of Synchronicity

What exactly is synchronicity? It is a concept first explained by psychiatrist Carl Jung who put forward the idea of events as "meaningful coincidences".

Synchronicity language is where information is exchanged via signs, coincidence and synchronicity and it is a common way through which our Guides or Higher Intelligence communicate.

We all experience synchronicity, yet many of us disregard it. If we do not recognize this type of communication as meaningful, it is easy to miss and dismiss the important messages it brings.

Some people know synchronicity is divine orchestration. That an intelligence and master plan lines up so called coincidences to communicate something significant.

Oprah Winfrey recently told a story of divine orchestration on the Dr. Oz television show. She shared the story of what convinced her to play the role of Henrietta's mother is the HBO film, 'Immortal Life of Henrietta Lacks'. Her story is unbelievable, no one could have designed it or orchestrated it. As I listened to these bizarre details, I felt overjoyed inside. I love how Oprah communicates so clearly the importance of "meaningful coincidences". If you would like to listen to the story, go to Dr. Oz youtube channel and type in 'Why Oprah Doesn't Believe in Coincidences'.

What 'meaningful coincidences' have appeared in your life? How can you become aware and notice more 'meaningful coincidences'?

Beliefs About Communication

What is your belief about communication? What do you believe must happen in order for you to consider it as communication?

Take a minute to evaluate your beliefs. Do you believe a conversation must include two people speaking the same language? Can you have a conversation with someone who speaks a different language? If you answer yes, how is it possible? Perhaps with hand gestures, pictures, or pointing to objects.

For example, if you are traveling to an international destination where the English language is not spoken and you want to find a tourist attraction, how can you go about getting that information? You could show a citizen of that country a picture of the location and gesture with your shoulders indicating you need help with directions. He or she could point you in the right direction or draw a map for you. You may not have exchanged words in the same language, however, you exchanged information and communicated.

This little example helps us discover we can be in communication with others regardless if we speak the same language.

What about communication that happens without verbal exchange? Do you believe people can communicate without voice exchange? Yes, you might be thinking about deaf people who communicate with their hands via sign language. Or you might be thinking of people who receive information with their finger tips, touching patterns of raised dots or braille.

These are a few examples to help us become aware of the multiple forms of expression or communication.

The Tremendous Power of Music

Some people connect with their Guides or Multidimensional Self through music.

One such friend, Dylan Mendicino, shared with me that he uses the guidance of music. He explained that when he listens to music, he hears, not only lyrics that seem important in the moment, but the music within the music that he's sure only he can hear.

He says it's like listening to singing in his head, except it's more angelic, honest and mesmerizing. How does this guide him? Well, he explains it's like that feeling you get when you hear a song that makes your day or turns a bad situation into a good one, except the timing is better and you can learn about yourself, others and reality from it.

He believes music does that for a lot of people, but when you delve into the spiritual side of music, even the astral, music is another level of consciousness that needs better appreciation and understanding. Its benefits are profound.

Embracing Intuition

We have all been touched by the spiritual realm at some point in our lives. There is a 'knowing' that we can't quite put our fingers on. So we either ignore it, or collapse into the comforting embrace of skepticism.

Skepticism or doubt are coping mechanisms that divide the world and its experiences into the rational and irrational. Reductive reasoning allows many of us to partition ourselves from the possibility of a spiritual dimension by rubbishing it as illogical. There are, though, so many sensations and experiences which scarcely find explanation in conventional learning.

For example, why do humans seem to have such a strong affinity for water? When we go on holiday, it's often to a destination with water. Many of us are positively drawn to lakes, the seashore or even a riverbank. Biologically, this is peculiar because human beings have absolutely no natural adaptations for aquatic or marine environments.

Think about it, we aren't born swimmers nor can we extract oxygen from water to breathe. Of course, water sustains life, but for a great many people, being on or around the water sustains and nourishes the soul. Many of you might be hard pressed to explain why that is, but you don't question it. You yield unfailingly the call of the water.

Many of us do things without understanding why. I hope this book has given you some insight into how to make sense of the otherworldly promptings we all experience in life. We all have the tools to access a higher form of consciousness; all that's needed is an openness to our Guides and our Multidimensional Selves. You too can answer that call of the water...the call of intuition.

The next time you hear your phone ring and energetically you sense it is Intuition calling, will you be inspired to answer? Will curiosity allow you to investigate what information Intuition might be wanting to share?

www.ingramcontent.com/pod-product-compliance
Lightning Source LLC
Chambersburg PA
CBHW060605030426
42337CB00019B/3608